Becoming a Successful Supervisor

Develop essential people skills

Rick Conlow
Doug Watsabaugh

Viva Books
New Delhi | Mumbai | Chennai | Kolkata
Bengaluru | Hyderabad | Kochi | Guwahati

First Indian Edition 2011

VIVA BOOKS PRIVATE LIMITED

- 4737/23 Ansari Road, Daryaganj, New Delhi 110 002
  E-mail: vivadelhi@vivagroupindia.net, Tel. 42242200
- 76, Service Industries, Shirvane, Sector 1, Nerul, Navi Mumbai 400 706
  E-mail: vivamumbai@vivagroupindia.net, Tel. 27721273, 27721274
- Jamals Fazal Chambers, 26 Greams Road, Chennai 600 006
  E-mail: vivachennai@vivagroupindia.net, Tel. 28290304, 28294241
- B-103, Jindal Towers, 21/1A/3 Darga Road, Kolkata 700 017
  E-mail: vivakolkata@vivagroupindia.net, Tel. 22836381, 22816713
- 7, Sovereign Park Apartments, 56-58, K. R. Road, Basavanagudi, Bengaluru 560 004
  E-mail: vivabangalore@vivagroupindia.net, Tel. 26607409, 26607410
- 101-102 Mughal Marc Aptt., 3-4-637 to 641, Narayanguda, Hyderabad 500 029
  E-mail: vivahyderabad@vivagroupindia.net, Tel. 27564481, 27564482
- First Floor, Beevi Towers, SRM Road, Kaloor, Kochi 682 018, Kerala
  E-mail: vivakochi@vivagroupindia.net, Tel: 0484-2403055, 2403056
- 232, GNB Road, Beside UCO Bank, Silpukhuri, Guwahati 781 003
  E-mail: vivaguwahati@vivagroupindia.net, Tel: 0361-2666386

www.vivagroupindia.com

Published by arrangement with

Axzo Press, LLC
562, Willow Brook Office Park
Fairport, New York 14450

ISBN : 978-81-309-1831-0

Published by Vinod Vasishtha for Viva Books Private Limited, 4737/23, Ansari Road, Daryaganj, New Delhi - 110 002. Printed and bound by Raj Press, R-3, Inderpuri, New Delhi - 110 012.

Table of Contents

About the Author

Rick Conlow

A quick glance at his professional resume leaves you with the strong impression that effort and optimism are a winning combination. Case in point: With Rick by their side, clients have achieved double- and triple-digit improvement in their sales performance, quality, customer loyalty, and service results over the past 20-plus years and earned more than 30 quality and service awards.

In a day and age when optimism and going the extra mile can sound trite, Rick has made them a differentiator. His clients include organizations that are leaders in their industries, as well as others that are less recognizable. Regardless, their goals are his goals.

Rick's life view and extensive background in sales and leadership—as a general manager, vice president, training director, program director, national sales trainer and consultant—are the foundation of his coaching, training, and consulting services. Participants in Rick's experiential "live action" programs walk away with ah-has, inspiration, and skills they can immediately put to use.

These programs include "BEST Selling!"; "Moments of Magic!"; "Excellence in Management!"; "SuperSTAR Service and Selling!"; "The Greatest Secrets of all Time!"; and "Good Boss/Bad Boss—Which One Are You?"

Rick has also authored *Excellence in Management, Excellence in Supervision, Returning to Learning,* and *Moments of Magic.*

When he's not engaging an audience or engrossed in a coaching discussion, this proud husband and father is most likely astride a weight bench or motorcycle, taking on the back roads and highways of Minnesota.

Doug Watsabaugh

Doug values being a "regular person," with his feet on the ground and head in the realities of the daily challenges his clients face. It's his heart for and experience in helping clients deal with difficult situations that distinguish him from other sales performance and leadership development consultants.

His knowledge of experiential learning and his skill at designing change processes and learning events have enabled him to measurably improve the lives of thousands of individuals and hundreds of organizations in a wide variety of industries—financial services, manufacturing, medical devices, consumer goods, and technology to name a few.

Before starting his own business, Doug served as the director of operations for a national training institute, manager of organization development for a major chemical company, and was responsible for worldwide training and organization development for the world's third largest toy company.

He was also a partner in Performance & Human Development LLC, a California company that published high-involvement experiential activities, surveys and instruments, interactive training modules, papers, and multimedia presentations.

Doug has co-authored two books with John E. Jones, Ph.D., and William L. Bearley, Ed. D.: *The New Fieldbook for Trainers* published by HRD Press and Lakewood Publishing, and *The OUS Quality Item Pool,* about organizational survey items that measure Baldrige criteria.

He is a member of the American Society for Training and Development (ASTD), the Minnesota Quality Council, and The National Organization Development Network.

Doug's father taught him the value of hard work, and it paid dividends: He funded his college education playing guitar and singing with a rock 'n' roll band, experiencing a close call with fame when he played bass in concert with Chuck Berry. Not bad for a guy who admits to being "a bit shy."

While Doug's guitar remains a source of enjoyment, it pales in comparison to his "number one joy and priority"—his family.

WCW Partners

WCW Partners is a performance improvement company, with more than 20 years of experience helping companies, governmental agencies, and nonprofit organizations worldwide revitalize their results and achieve record-breaking performance.

We are experts in sales performance, organization development, leadership development, marketing and communications—and we don't mind telling you that we're different than most consulting firms you'll find in the marketplace.

For one thing, it's our approach—when you hire us, you get us. But just as important, we're people who've had to wrestle with the same issues you have—how to strengthen sales, boost productivity, improve quality, increase employee satisfaction, build a team, or retain and attract new customers. To us, "We develop the capability in you" is more than a catchy phrase. It's our promise.

Our clients include 3M, American Express, American Medical Systems, Amgen Inc., Accenture, AmeriPride Services, Andersen Windows, Avanade, Beltone, Canadian Linen and Uniform Service, Carew International, Case Corporation, Citigroup, Coca-Cola, Costco, Covance, Deknatel, Eaton Corporation, Electrochemicals Inc., Entergy, Esoterix, General Mills, GN Resound, Grant Thornton, Hasbro Inc., Honeywell, Interton, Kenner Products, Marketlink, Kemps-Marigold, Meijer Corporation, National Computer Systems, Parker Brothers, Toro, Productive Workplace Systems, Red Wing Shoes, Rite Aid, Rollerblade, Ryan Companies, Travelers Insurance, Thrivent, Tonka Corporation, and a number of nonprofit and educational institutions.

To learn how you can do amazing things, visit us on line at WCWPartners.com or contact Doug or Rick toll free at 1-888-313-0514.

Preface

So you're about to become a supervisor for the first time, or have recently become one. You probably have mixed emotions. On one hand, you're excited about the opportunities. You'll be able to help and work with employees as no supervisor ever did with you! Yet, you also have concerns. Can you do it? How will your new peers accept you? What will the employees, some of them friends, think of you now? Where do you start?

Whatever your emotions, they're okay. It's not unusual to have some reservations while you look forward to the job. The good news is that *Becoming a Successful Supervisor* will be a big help. In addition, two of the other books in our Crisp Supervisory Series will help you as well. Consider reading and working your way through *Achieving Supervisory Excellence* and *Creating a High Performing Team* as well. Both will provide helpful tips and tools to propel you on your way to success.

As a supervisor, you'll lead other people. As a leader, always remember that your employees' success is your success. You may still be required to do some of the tasks that the employees do; however, you'll also be responsible for getting things done through others. You won't be able to do it all alone.

This book is dedicated to helping you quickly learn and immediately apply the people skills of supervising. Most supervisors who fail do so because they are inexperienced in the people-handling skills, not because they lack technical job skills. The five parts of the book outline and describe the critical success factors you need to create a positive, powerful, motivating environment for your employees. You will be challenged with application exercises to put the strategies discussed into practice. At the end of each section, you will review key strategies and include them in your action planning.

It's been said that winning isn't everything; the will to prepare to win is everything. Achieving excellence means knowing and doing those things that others are unwilling to learn or act on. Now, let's get started!

Positively,

Doug Watsabaugh and Rick Conlow

How Many Squares Do You See?

At first glance, most people see 16 or 17. By continuing to look at the image, you'll see that there are 30 squares.

At first glance, you may recognize only a small percentage of your potential as a supervisor. With commitment, training, and persistence, you'll be able to reach a position of excellence in supervision. Now, let's make it happen!

Learning Objectives

Complete this book, and you'll know how to:

1) Transition to a supervisory role.
2) Apply the principles and processes of high performance management.
3) Proactively communicate with others.
4) Use effective coaching skills to achieve increased employee satisfaction and productivity.
5) Acquire strategies for dealing with organizational change.

Workplace and Management Competencies mapping

For over 30 years, business and industry has utilized competency models to select employees. The trend to use competency-based approaches in education and training, assessment, and development of workers has experienced a more recent emergence within the Employment and Training Administration (ETA), a division of the United States Department of Labor.

The ETA's General Competency Model Framework spans a wide array of competencies from the more basic competencies, such as reading and writing, to more advanced occupation-specific competencies. The Viva-Crisp Series finds its home in what the ETA refers to as the Workplace Competencies and the Management Competencies.

Becoming a Successful Supervisor covers information vital to mastering the following competencies:

Workplace Competencies:

- Teamwork

Management Competencies:

- Supporting Others
- Motivating & Inspiring

About the Viva-Crisp 50-Minute Series

The Viva-Crisp 50-Minute Series was designed to cover critical business and professional development topics in the shortest possible time. Our easy-to-read, easy-to-understand format can be used for self-study or for classroom training. With a wealth of hands-on exercises, the 50-Minute books keep you engaged and help you retain critical skills.

What You Need to Know

We designed the Viva-Crisp 50-Minute Series to be as self-explanatory as possible. But there are a few things you should know before you begin the book.

Exercises

Exercises look like this:

EXERCISE TITLE

Questions and other information would be here.

Keep a pencil handy. Any time you see an exercise, you should try to complete it. If the exercise has specific answers, an answer key will be provided in the appendix. (Some exercises ask you to think about your own opinions or situation; these types of exercises will not have answer keys.)

Forms

A heading like this means that the rest of the page is a form:

FORMHEAD

Forms are meant to be reusable. You might want to make a photocopy of a form before you fill it out, so that you can use it again later.

A Note to Instructors

We've tried to make the Viva-Crisp 50-Minute Series books as useful as possible as classroom training manuals. Here arc some of the features we provide for instructors:

- PowerPoint presentations
- Answer keys
- Assessments
- Customization

PowerPoint Presentations

You can download a PowerPoint presentation for this book from our Web site at www.CrispSeries.com.

Answer keys

If an exercise has specific answers, an answer key will be provided in the appendix. (Some exercises ask you to think about your own opinions or situation; these types of exercises will not have answer keys.)

PART 1

Transitioning to Supervision

"*When you're accustomed to doing stand-up, so often you're the only person onstage and it's all your thing. It's very gladiatorial. Obviously, when you're in a scene with somebody, you're supposed to listen and react—and that's a bit of a transition.*"

–**Jon Stewart**

In this part:

- You'll discover how your role has changed and learn some strategies and tips to make the transition successfully.
- You'll get an overview of the new competencies you'll need to be successful. You'll get a tool to assess your planning for future development.
- You'll discover how your current use of time reflects your view of your role. This activity will give you a chance to make choices that guide your future in your new role.
- You'll develop an action plan to put you on the road to success.

The Opportunity

You are in for an exciting journey. As a rule, supervisors have more responsibility and make more money than other employees. They also have more work and greater stress. Supervisory positions are challenging because you are responsible for more results even though you don't do all the jobs. That's the opportunity. If you can improve performance through your efforts with a small group, you can do it with larger groups as you learn more, develop your skills, and progress in your career.

WHY DO YOU WANT TO SUPERVISE OTHERS?

Check all that apply.

____ To increase your job satisfaction

____ To challenge your skills

____ To learn and grow

____ To gain more responsibility

____ To make more money

____ To achieve a personal goal

____ To gain confidence

____ Other: ____

Make no mistake about it, there will be problems. A new supervisor called one of his close friends after work one night and said, "Bill, I can't stand it. Every day, people are late or absent. And it seems like the quality of their work is so poor. And, when I try to get them to do better, they won't listen to me. What's the matter with these employees? I don't know if I'm cut out for this."

You can tell that this new supervisor is frustrated. Many people become supervisors because of the skill or experience they acquired. They are often surprised to find that supervising is a whole new job. It requires different skills, and the satisfaction comes from different places. In short, it is a different ballgame than just doing the work. The skills can be learned—you can learn them from this book. These skills include working with people, communicating well with others, using performance management skills, effectively coaching others, and handling change positively.

Your Role Changes Now

You were a successful individual contributor before this promotion. You may have been a model of success for others in your department or company. Similar success as an individual contributor has been a stumbling block for many as they make the transition to their new role as a supervisor. Here are some ways your role changes when you become a supervisor:

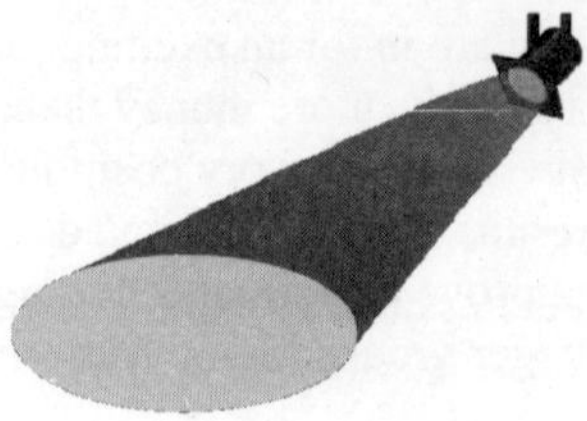

1 **From me to we.** As an individual contributor, you had wide latitude in the use of your time, the approach to your tasks, and a great deal of control over your job and how you did it. Now you are responsible for the work of everyone on your team. You must ensure that the work of your team meets the needs of the organization and its customers. Timing, style, priority conflicts, work quality, and many other variables are now your responsibility.

2 **You now speak for the organization.** As an individual contributor, you can speculate, speak your thoughts out loud, and for the most part, you can say anything you want as long as it doesn't violate laws or company policy. As a supervisor, your employees may believe what you say or write and assume that it represents the "voice of the company." Inappropriate or inaccurate information from you can set off wide-spread uncertainty, anger, or fear. It may waste time, effort, and money.

3 **You now have responsibility for the most important asset of the company—its people.** The supervisor is the most important source of communication from the company. As the supervisor, you impact the quality of work life as well as the physical and emotional well-being of your employees. You can contribute positively or negatively to employee morale and organizational life.

4 **You now have position power.** As the supervisor you have an impact because you are the boss. You always had power—the power of your knowledge, expertise, personality, and so on. You still have that personal power but you'll need to get used to the (positive and negative) impact of your position power. And you'll need to be thoughtful about how you choose to use it.

SUPERVISORY SKILLS SELF-ASSESSMENT

As a supervisor, you have an obligation to provide leadership, information, and service to your internal customers—your subordinates and peers. Use this assessment to begin planning your transition to supervisor. Use the scale below to rate yourself in each of these behaviors.

1 = Not at all; 2 = Very mildly; 3 = Mildly; 4 = Somewhat; 5 = Very; 6 = Extremely

____ 1. Working effectively with others to develop a common vision for the future

____ 2. Translating organizational goals into clear objectives for your group

____ 3. Developing clear performance objectives for your employees

____ 4. Effectively communicating your goals and objectives

____ 5. Maintaining performance standards for your employees

____ = **Total: Developing Clear Expectations (1–5)**

____ 6. Delegating tasks appropriately

____ 7. Monitoring the task performance of subordinates

____ 8. Recognizing effective employee performance

____ 9. Redirecting employee behavior that produces ineffective results

10. Coaching others in developing skills

____ 11. Regularly giving performance feedback based on clear expectations

____ 12. Adapting leadership to the needs of individuals

____ 13. Conducting performance appraisals effectively

____ = **Total: Coaching for Excellence (6–13)**

CONTINUED

CONTINUED

____ 14. Appropriately recognizing employees for their accomplishments

____ 15. Connecting your performance expectations to employee values

____ 16. Motivating others effectively

____ 17. Assigning work that is appropriately challenging to meet employee development needs

____ 18. Using subordinate suggestions well

____ = **Total: Communication and Motivation (14–18)**

____ 19. Involving others appropriately in decisions that affect them

____ 20. Promoting effective teamwork

____ 21. Treating others fairly

____ 22. Creating an environment free from fear and punishment

____ 23. Working well with others

____ 24. Treating mistakes as opportunities for learning

____ 25. Confronting behavior that contradicts your organizations values

____ = **Total: Employee Engagement and Productive Climate (19–25)**

Supervisory Skills Self-Assessment Scoring

Write your score for each area in the Score column and then check the box that corresponds with your score. Then move on to the Action Planning Guide.

Items	Measures	Score
1–5	**Developing Clear Expectations:** Your ability to create clear objectives and communicate expectations that focus group and individual employees on the organization's needs.	Area score total: _____ ❑ 23–30 Highly developed ❑ 15–22 Improvement suggested ❑ 5–14 Immediate work needed
6–13	**Coaching for Excellence:** Your ability to delegate, adapt your leadership style, coach, and communicate to ensure the growth and success of your employees. Includes hiring thru performance appraisals.	Area score total: _____ ❑ 37–48 Highly developed ❑ 22–36 Improvement suggested ❑ 8–21 Immediate work needed
14–18	**Communication and Motivation:** Your ability to engage employees, inspire them to higher levels of performance, recognize their contributions and reward their accomplishments.	Area score total: _____ ❑ 23–30 Highly developed ❑ 15–22 Improvement suggested ❑ 5–14 Immediate work needed
19–25	**Employee Engagement and Productive Climate:** The degree to which you build a climate that supports appropriate individual responsibility, risk taking and commitment to constructive behavioral norms that support the organization's values.	Area score total: _____ ❑ 33–42 Highly developed ❑ 20–32 Improvement suggested ❑ 7–19 Immediate work needed

ACTION PLANNING GUIDE

1. List areas from the survey that are clearly growth opportunities for you:

2. From the list of growth opportunities, choose two or three that will provide the biggest payoff for you right now:

3. What's the payoff for you to grow in these areas?

4. What have you tried before? What worked?

5. What resources are available to support you in these developmental opportunities?

6. What do you intend to do first?

7. Who needs to know about this?

8. How will you enlist others to help you?

How You Use Your Time

Planning can ensure that you get off to a good start in your new role, and avoid transition issues that are common to a new supervisory role. The way you currently use your time is a good indicator of how you view your job. Let's take a look at how you are currently using your time.

1. **Doing the job:** acting as an individual contributor—doing the job you did before you were promoted.
2. **Fulfilling administrative tasks:** Doing paperwork, managing budgets, answering email, participating in management meetings, and so on.
3. **Engaging/Communicating with your team:** Setting expectations and direction, coaching for improved performance, problem solving, and providing performance support.
4. **Serving your customer(s):** Meeting/working with your internal and/or external customers. Staying in touch with their needs and ensuring their satisfaction and loyalty.

"Hey, you're the boss… it's not like if I screw up you're going to eat me."

CASE STUDY: Jake on the Job

Jake's continued good performance in his job earned him the notice of upper management. When a supervisor role became available in his department, Jake was promoted. A review of how Jake uses his time revealed the following:

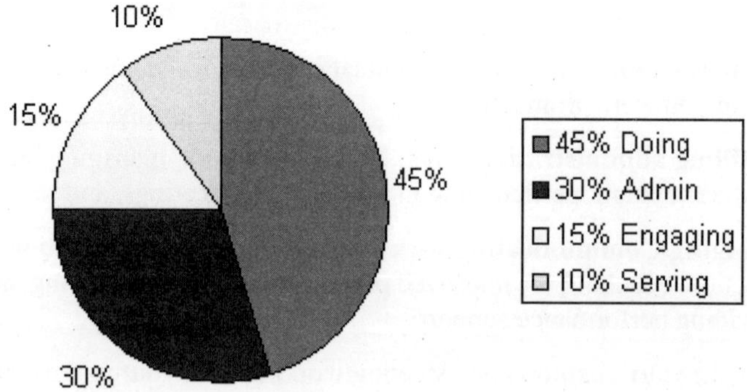

Current Use of Time

Review Jake's chart. Observe that the amount of time spent doing the job and conducting administrative activities is very large. And, notice that the amount of time spent engaging with the team and serving customers is relatively small. This is a problem for Jake, although he is hardly alone. This is a common problem with people who have just transitioned to a supervisory role.

Management Time

Use the pie chart below to represent how you currently use time. Use the categories listed and draw them into the chart. Set the size of the pie chart slices to match the amount of your time you actually use in each category.

How I Use My Time

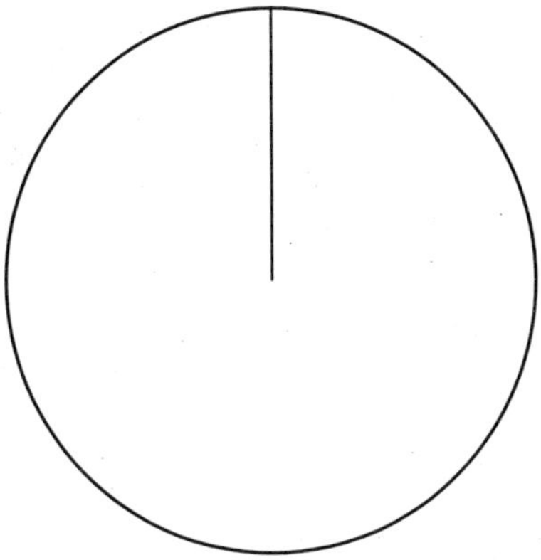

______ % Doing my old job

______ % Doing admin work

______ % Engaging with my team

______ % Serving my customers

Review

Examine your pie chart and determine if the way you're using your time represents the ideal profile for your new role. Are you sending too much of your time doing your old job? Are you spending too much of your time on your computer, or in your office isolated from your team? Would you benefit from changing toward more significant supervisory activity? Use the Time Usage Inventory that follows to make those decisions.

TIME USAGE INVENTORY

Use this exercise to decide how to perform more effectively in your new role.

	T	F
1. I will benefit by doing less "individual contributor" work.	❑	❑
2. I will benefit by spending less time in my office doing administrative work when my team is available for interaction.	❑	❑
3. I will benefit by increasing the amount of time I spend with my team (coaching, solving problems, clarifying, and so on).	❑	❑
4. I will benefit by increasing the amount of time I spend with our customers (internal and/or external).	❑	❑

Based on your responses to the questions above, use the pie chart below to divide the use of your time into the "ideal" slices of time.

How I Will Use My Supervisory Time

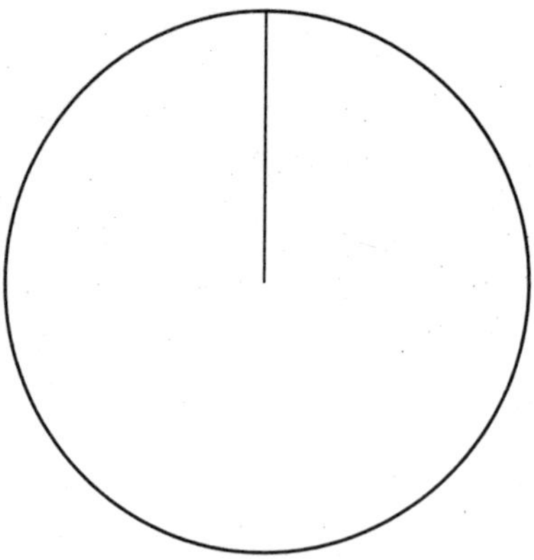

_______ % Individual contributor

_______ % Admin work

_______ % With my team

_______ % With our customers

Transition Speed Bumps

CASE STUDY: Roger's Reign

Roger, a financial analyst, was a rising star in the finance department. He was tapped to fill a supervisory role that opened up when a supervisor took a position at another company. Roger had an MBA and had worked in the finance department for three years.

After Roger had been on the job for three weeks, employees began complaining to human resources about changes Roger was making.

- He told all members of the group that "things are going to change around here."
- He arbitrarily rearranged work assignments.
- Two employees were placed on probationary status.
- All employees were told that they weren't working hard enough.
- Roger told members of the group they needed to put in more hours.
- He announced that he was going to promote an employee whom everyone knew to be his best friend.

Employees in the group told HR that they were working for the boss from hell. On the job, they assumed a defensive posture. Productivity declined as they focused on their perceived mistreatment. At an off-site lunchtime meeting they decided to take their concerns to Roger's manager.

This case study is a composite of commonplace missteps by a new supervisor. Roger's situation is not that unusual. When moving into a new role, there are some speed bumps that you can avoid with a bit of foresight and planning.

- Start the job by taking some time to examine this significant transition. Gain some perspective on yourself and the requirements of the job. Plan how you're going to approach the job. Without that perspective and planning, you may get swept along by the immediate challenges of the new position. You might let current, urgent demands prevent you from planning efforts to address long-term priorities.
- Don't assume your job is to just keep things running smoothly. Your job is to move things forward. Initiate productive change; improve efficiencies, and overcome past problems or deficiencies in the department. You must gain perspective from your superiors and others around you about the expectations for your department or group.

- Don't assume everyone sees the same problems and need for change you do. Making those changes unilaterally from your position of power will generate resistance and reduce employee trust and commitment.

- You may find it uncomfortable to give others direction, and you may think it's easier to just do things yourself. If you do, you further isolate yourself from your team, and you end up acting as an individual contributor instead of a supervisor. This is not why you were promoted.

- You must become comfortable communicating your needs, running meetings, giving feedback, meeting individually, or conducting other communication activities. If not, your employees will feel isolated from you and disconnected from the steps they need to take to fulfill expectations. You may end up feeling unsupported and unable to ask for the help you need to succeed.

- Your former peers—now your employees—will treat you differently. You are the same person, so you might assume the relationships haven't changed. But some employees take an "us and them" approach to peers vs. managers, and you are now one of "them." These relationships are further complicated if you are supervising people who wanted your job. Former peers may feel that you have forgotten where you came from.

- Your work demands will pick up dramatically. Many new supervisors are surprised by the sheer number of meetings they are expected to attend and the number of communications they get on a daily basis. For most supervisors the work load continues to grow and accelerate.

So, Now What?

Four steps:

1. Clarify expectations.
2. Assess your strengths.
3. Develop a transition plan.
4. Implement your plan.

Clarify Expectations

Ensure that you understand the organization's expectations, whether or not you knew they were there. The organization's leaders may have changed strategies. New strategies may be based on the expectation that the work of your department will change or improve now that you are in command. Acknowledge your own personal goals. Check with key stakeholders to determine what changes are necessary or desirable. Do your own assessment and develop a vision and goals for the group's future.

Assess Your Strengths

Assess your personal strengths to determine your development needs. Decide what you need to do to further develop your skills, and how you can call on your team to fill in where your strengths are lacking. It's also important to determine what you and others expect of your department. This will allow you to set appropriate performance goals and targets.

Develop a Transition Plan

Your transition plan should begin after your assessments are complete. Get to know your team. Learn their strengths and weaknesses and build the relationships needed for you to help them to be successful. Your plan should include clear statements of the results you want to produce in addition to milestones along the way. Don't forget to include your team in your assessment of its performance, and ask for their ideas about possible changes.

Implement Your Plan

Shape your role with a focus on the needs of the group to successfully meet the objectives you established. Place particular emphasis on team communication, coaching, and support for group performance. Ensure that you take care of yourself and get the support you need from superiors in the organization to enable success

Plan for the Change

Your transition begins with the ending of your old job. Once you step into your new role, you may experience feelings of disorientation, and you may even find yourself wondering if it was a mistake to take the job. Your new beginning will take hold when you have a clear sense of what you're doing, and you begin to settle into the new routine. Use the form that follows to develop a roadmap for your first few months. Plan to build new relationships with your team and to learn about the new job and department. Assess your talent pool and the direction and quality of work produced by your group. Decide where your strengths and development needs reside and how to apply them to upgrade the quality of your staff and their work. The clearer your focus, the easier it will be to communicate to get those results, and to adjust in process.

> ***"In the long run, men hit only what they aim at. Therefore, though they should fail immediately, they had better aim at something high."***
>
> **–Henry David Thoreau**

TRANSITION PLAN

Goal

____

____

Action Steps

1. ____________________________________
2. ____________________________________
3. ____________________________________
4. ____________________________________
5. ____________________________________

Success Criteria

- ▶ ____________________________________
- ▶ ____________________________________
- ▶ ____________________________________
- ▶ ____________________________________

Expected Outcome

____

____

____

Working Successfully with People

Suggested Strategies

Each part of this book has suggested strategies followed by action planning at the end. The strategies and planning are designed to help you prepare to win, get started the right way, and achieve excellence in supervision.

STRATEGIES FOR TRANSITION

1. Obtain a copy of your job description. Read it and then discuss it thoroughly with your boss. Use it to clarify expectations, goals, plans, and priorities.
2. Interview three other supervisors that you admire. Include only one in your current company so you obtain perceptions that are different than your current situation. Along with other concerns you have, ask them how they:
    - ▷ Motivate people
    - ▷ Handle problems
    - ▷ Keep a good attitude
3. Make a plan to complete this book thoroughly and act on its strategies. Then make a commitment to keep learning. Over the next 6 to12 months, attend two seminars and read three other Crisp books, including *Excellence in Management*. Refer to the book list in the Appendix for more ideas.
4. Develop a written plan for your work area. Outline your priorities, the goals needed to achieve those priorities, and the action steps to be taken toward those goals. Review this with someone close to you for objective feedback. Then ask your boss for a meeting to discuss it, and make any needed adjustments. If you aren't a supervisor yet, focus on getting there.
5. Meet with your boss a couple of times a month for 30 to 60 minutes to review results. Update your manager on your progress. Discuss problems you're facing, and your ideas and plans to resolve them. Get input and new information from your boss. If your manager doesn't initiate progress review meetings, request them in a positive way. If your boss won't take time to do this, find another supervisor that you respect, inside or outside your company, to review your progress and difficulties. It will help you focus, maintain a good attitude, and keep improving.

Part Summary

In this part, we've discussed the realities of the transition to supervision, and we've identified key competencies you'll need for success. We've also given you an opportunity to do a self check on your current skill with these competencies. With that information, you've planned your focus for the future to develop the skills and use your time most effectively to make a successful transition to supervision.

P A R T 2

High-Performance Management

> "*Excellence in supervision is not 'what you know.' It's what you do with what you know.*"
>
> –**Rick Conlow**

In this part:

- You'll learn how to use the High Performance Equation to guide you in planning and carrying out effective supervisory activities in your new role.
- You'll learn how to package and deliver clear performance expectations to your team.
- You'll learn how to deliver motivational positive feedback.
- You'll receive guidance on coaching employees to higher performance.
- You'll get help with how to handle difficult situations, such as employee discipline and performance appraisal.

Performance Management

How do I motivate people? And, how do I handle performance problems? These are the most commonly asked questions by supervisors and managers. The answers are the key to managing for high performance.

All people are motivated. It's just that some people aren't motivated to do what *you* want them to do. Practical experience and research give clues to key performance management skills. They are:

- Set clear expectations and goals.
- Give positive recognition and praise.
- Handle performance problems effectively.
- Supervise with flexibility.

The High Performance Equation

The High Performance Equation can be expressed as a formula in which:

$$HP = E^{C} x\, (C + M + E)$$

HP = High Performance

Every organization needs high performance from its workforce. It is the responsibility of the supervisor to ensure those results. This means increasing productivity, improving quality, increasing sales, and increasing customer satisfaction are the outcomes supervisors try to accomplish.

E^{C} = Clear Expectations

In our experience, fully 80% of performance problems are a result of a lack of clear expectations. Supervisors often assume employees know what is expected. These assumptions often result in disappointment for both the supervisor and the employee. Supervisors often communicate incomplete or vague instructions, and assume the employee will know what a good job looks like. Goals and objectives must be thought through carefully, and communicated clearly to ensure high performance results.

C = Competence

Employees must have the ability to do the job. Competence is made up of skills; knowledge and experience provide the know-how and the can-do for success. Willingness and desire alone cannot substitute for competence.

M = Motivation

Employees must also have the willingness, desire, and confidence to produce high performance. "Want to" combined with "can-do" contributes to high performance. The world is full of competent people who have no desire to do certain tasks. Competence produces nothing without motivation.

E = Environment

Consider the impact of the organization's climate, work group norms, and management style on the performance of employees. Environment is reflected in the degree to which employees feel supported in their efforts to perform their job. Employees need support for reasonable risk-taking, decision-making, and personal accountability. Environment also defines how mistakes on the job are treated. Employees punished for making a mistake will become overly cautious and risk-averse. Treat mistakes as learning opportunities.

Summary

High-performance management begins with establishment of **clear expectations** for results, and is supported by employee **competence, motivation,** and a supportive **environment**. The high performance model provides direction for the supervisor role. An effective supervisor plans and communicates clear expectations. The supervisor must support employee growth and development to enhance competence and job skills. The supervisor must be able to appeal to employee interests and values and to inspire their desire and willingness to perform effectively.

> ***"No one ever accomplishes anything of consequence without a goal.... Goal setting is the strongest human force for self-actualization."***
>
> **–Paul Myer**

How to Establish Clear Expectations

Establish clear expectations by meeting with employees one-on-one. Consider a number of critical connections to properly set employee expectations, such as:

- Be certain that you understand your organization's objectives. Where is it trying to go in five years? Understand your business unit's objectives.
- Based on your organization's objectives, set your workgroup's objectives to move the organization forward.
- Review the employee's job description. Make sure it is current and that it fully describes the job. If there is no job description, write one. If it is outdated, develop a new one. Many organizations have human resource professionals who can be very helpful in developing the job description.
- Translate your workgroup and employee objectives into **SMART** objectives to ensure that employees understand their contribution. Help each employee see a link between their job and how it contributes to the organization's long-term objectives.

S. M. A. R. T. Objectives

Discuss performance goals and job standards during the employee meeting. For most jobs, you determine three to five job goals. A goal needs to be S.M.A.R.T:

Specific. An objective must be specific, not general. "Improve your communication" is not a useful statement of your expectations. Do you want improvement in written or oral communications? Should the employee become a better public speaker or use e-mail more effectively?

Measurable. How much or how many? What customers must be satisfied? What will success look like? What metrics are you using to determine how success and progress will be observed? Your measures give you and your employees a common view of progress achieved.

Attainable. The objective should be attainable with "stretch," meaning there should be some appropriate level of challenge to the successful achievement of the expectation. Too little stretch and the goal is too easily achieved. Too much stretch and the goal seems out of reach. Appropriate stretch challenges and motivates employees.

Relevant. An objective should be relevant to the business of the organization. It should make sense to the employee asked to perform the tasks.

Timed. The objective or task should be "time bound," meaning there is an expectation that it will be completed by a certain date. Timing may also involve a frequency or specified pace for accomplishment. Timing aligns expectations and provides an appropriate sense of urgency for the objective.

All good performance begins with clear expectations and goals. Without a clear understanding of expectations, employees seldom reach their potential. Unfortunately, nearly 7 out of 10 supervisors and managers fail at this. Excellent supervisors do it well, and so can you.

A customer service supervisor had poor customer survey results in his department. After attending a seminar, he refocused his performance management skills. He and his employees set customer satisfaction goals and installed a recognition plan to recognize progress and to reward accomplishment. After six months, the department's customer service ratings were better and employee morale improved as well.

One of the biggest obstacles supervisors have to deal with is the increasing demands on their time. Remember these two points:

- 80% of performance problems relate to a lack of clear expectations and goals.
- Research shows that effective performance goals can improve performance 25% in areas where it hasn't been applied.

Apply these principles as you fill out the form on the next page.

ESTABLISHING CLEAR EXPECTATIONS AND GOALS

Name: ______________________________

Job: ______________________________

Responsibilities: ______________________________

____

____

Key Duties: Mark priorities with an asterisk, mark strengths with a plus sign, and mark areas to improve with a check mark.

____

____

____

____

____

S. M. A. R. T. Performance Goals

____

____

____

____

____

____

____

____

____

____

____

Complete a copy of this form for each of your employees.

Giving Positive Feedback

It's been said that "feedback is the breakfast of champions." Feedback can be motivational or developmental. Both are critical tools for managing employee performance. Clearly, it is more pleasant to give and receive positive feedback. When done correctly, constructive developmental feedback can help employees better understand what is expected of them and how their actions contribute to success—for themselves and for the organization.

It all begins with positive recognition and praise. Over 90% of employees want more recognition. Have you ever received too much recognition? Here are the basic principles to keep in mind.

Principle	Examples
Be specific	*"Thanks for staying late..."*
Be as immediate as possible	*"Thanks for staying late tonight..."*
Relate the recognition to the activity/result	*"Thanks for staying late tonight to complete that rush order..."*
Relate the recognition to the person	*"Thanks for staying late tonight to complete that rush order, Bill..."*
Be sincere and genuine	*"Thanks for staying late tonight to complete that rush order, Bill. I appreciate it."*
Give weekly recognition	*"Good job meeting the deadline on that marketing plan this week."*
Praise progress, not just accomplishment	*"Your response times are getting closer to your goal and I appreciate how hard you are working on that."*

Positive feedback can include formal rewards and recognition, but be sure to follow the principles above. And, never assume the reward or recognition takes the place of specific, personalized praise. Be certain to tell the employee why he or she is being rewarded and add your sincere thanks.

Handling Performance Problems

At times you have to give developmental feedback. It's a key to high performance and motivation. If employees don't know when they're off track or don't realize they have made mistakes, how will they improve? For example, Olympic athletes get regular positive and negative feedback from their coaches during workouts.

As a general rule, there are no bad people, just some with behavior problems. An employee in a mechanical contracting company had a hard time completing important customer reports on time. In other areas of the job, he did fine. Just telling him to do it didn't change the behavior. Through regular review sessions in which his supervisor reviewed his performance and behavior, he improved.

Review sessions are one-on-one meetings for the purpose of giving direct developmental feedback to improve an employee's performance. A review session takes two general directions:

- **Counseling.** Use a mutual discussion process for occasional problems.
- **Disciplinary.** Use a directive process for chronic or ongoing problems.

Principles for Giving Constructive Feedback

When using either approach, keep the feedback simple and straightforward, and keep in mind the following principles:

- Be as immediate as possible.
- Be specific in describing the employee's behavior.
- Clarify your expectations, goals, and plans.
- Avoid judgmental criticism.
- Treat the person respectfully.

Counseling Process

Most employees want to do a good job. Some employees need extra help and sometimes they make mistakes. We're all human. In those instances, sit down with them privately and use these steps to help them get on track:

1. Identify the problem.

   "I want to talk to you about being late to work. This is unacceptable, because..."

2. Ask for the employee's view.

   "Please explain why this is happening."

3. Ask for ideas on how to improve or address the problem. Add your guidance.

   Ask: "What can you do to improve?" "What else can you do?"

   Offer: "What if you try..."

4. Agree on a plan, and then put it in writing.

   "So, the plan we discussed is ...

5. Establish a follow-up date for a review of the results of the plan.

   "Let's discuss results next week. Same time and place."

This process needs to be managed with two-way communication. Conduct it in a positive way. Be constructive, not critical. Focus on the problem but do not threaten the employee's self-esteem. Avoid judgmental comments such as, "It's stupid to do what you do," or "You're a lousy employee because of this."

"Hey, wake up, it's time to work."

Discipline Process

At times, it seems that nothing you do—goals, recognition, one-on-ones, feedback communication, or even counseling—seems to help an employee improve. Sometimes employees violate company policies or engage in unethical or illegal behavior. You may need to discipline the employee and even terminate their employment.

Your company probably has a disciplinary process. You must understand and follow it carefully. Most disciplinary processes include verbal and written warnings prior to actual termination. Here are the steps to follow in most cases:

1. Identify the problem.

   "Sara, the reason I want to talk with you is because your service contracts are below the performance standards we established and agreed to. We have talked about this before and we have created plans for improvement. Your efforts to improve and meet those standards have not been successful."

2. State the expectation or goal.

   "As you know, the goal and standards we focus on is..."

3. State the consequence.

   "Because of your sub-par poor performance, I'm giving you this reprimand, which I'm also documenting in your file. Continued poor performance could lead to termination."

4. Ask for employee comments; then summarize.

   "Sara, what we have discussed is.... I believe you can do this, and my hope is that you improve."

When you get to this stage, make certain that you

- Clearly understand company policies regarding discipline and termination. If not, get help from the human resources department or your manager.
- Talk things over with human resources and your manager.
- Are consistent and clear in setting expectations and goals, giving feedback, providing training, and communicating with the employee.

Discipline issues are serious for the employee and you. The employee's livelihood and self-esteem are at stake. The potential turnover can cause your company lost productivity, low morale, and wasted training dollars. Be sensitive, seek guidance, but also take action.

Supervising with Flexibility

Supervising with flexibility means working with employees according to their needs and situation. Remember that all employees need goals, recognition, and help with performance problems. Although you must apply your approach and company policies fairly, you will need to supervise people differently to help them perform at their best. For example, some employees need more training than others, some employees need more "pats on the back" or recognition, and a few require a lot more direction. Behavioral scientist Dr. Ken Blanchard calls it, "Different strokes for different folks." The first step involves analyzing an employee in two areas:

Motivation

This describes a person's willingness and desire to do the job. Does the employee want to do the job—and believe she can?

Skill

Sometimes skill is a function of job experience. Does the employee have the skill, knowledge, and ability to perform well?

As a supervisor, your job is to help enhance employees' willingness and ability to perform the job successfully. As we've already discussed, you can help employees increase their motivation and skills by setting expectations and goals, giving direction, and providing feedback. Another key to excellence in supervision is flexibility: determining how to best help each employee, according to the individual's current needs and situation. As you gain experience, you will develop a variety of tools and techniques that work for you. Initially, however, you can apply two basic approaches for managing high performance: the Relationship Approach (RA) and the Training Approach (TA).

Relationship Approach

There will be times when nothing you do as a supervisor seems to improve an employee's negative attitude. You won't win them all. But never underestimate the ability of an excellent supervisor to make a positive impact. That's a person who positively improves the performance of a department or work group and is invaluable to the company. Excellent supervisors apply the right approaches that motivate and train their people for greater success.

A new supervisor was asked once by the president of his company, "How do you motivate people?" He responded by saying, "All people motivate themselves, for their own goals. However, I will create an atmosphere in my area that helps employees decide to be excited and motivated to reach our department goals." The president was pleased with the supervisor's perspective. The Relationship Approach creates a positive and motivating work environment by building a genuine relationship with employees by getting to know them and understanding what they value and care about. This focuses more on the person's motivation than their skill. You spend more time encouraging and supporting than training.

The best supervisors use goals, performance counseling, and recognition as key strategies with all employees. They also seek to better understand each individual. What is their hot button? In other words, what motivates them? For example, if it is fishing, ask them about it once in a while. Other actions to take include:

- Encourage the employee.
- Ask for input. (Listen to the employee's ideas.)
- Solve problems with the employee.
- Be positive and enthusiastic.
- Check in with the person every day.
- Give regular praise.

Understanding Employee Needs

A survey in *Total Quality Newsletter* found people to be motivated by these top issues:

1. Challenge (goals, risks, change, learning)
2. Recognition for a job well done
3. A feeling of being in on things (teamwork, input, opportunity)
4. Job security
5. Money

Unfortunately, most supervisors and managers think money is the most important motivator. As a supervisor, focus on the top three areas listed above and you will cultivate a highly motivated, high-performing group. You will find that even your most experienced employees can reach new levels of accomplishment when you help renew their enthusiasm by meeting these needs and by building trust.

Training Approach

A supervisor is often required to do mostly on-the-job training (OJT) for employees who lack experience. With OJT, you invest more time in training and less on motivation.

OJT begins with clear expectations and goals. Then the supervisor or another lead employee teaches and guides the inexperienced employee on how to do a job or task. A lead employee is highly skilled and wants to help others learn.

P3 + E = Effective OJT

The four phases of effective OJT are abbreviated P3+E.

Present. Describe in detail how to do the job or task. Give an overview of the process; then describe each step. Provide written instructions or procedures. Finally, demonstrate how to do it as you explain the steps again. Be clear about what success looks like.

Practice. Give the employee an opportunity to try the task, preferably one step at a time. Provide encouragement and correct any mistakes. Include enough practice to ensure that the employee is able to complete it successfully several times. Then move on to the next task or training phase.

Perform. Allow the employee a trial to perform solo. Do this for a reasonable period of time.

\+

Evaluate. After the trial period, review results. Point out the positives and correct any errors constructively. If the employee needs more training, start over with the Present phase. If not, extend the trial period or begin training on a new task or goal.

Many supervisors go directly from Present to Perform, which isn't effective.

Excellent supervisors encourage employees to participate in company sponsored training. If your company offers courses or sends employees to outside programs, encourage employees to participate. Encourage their involvement in two to four sessions a year if possible. While this may leave you temporarily shorthanded in the near term, in the long term your employees will perform better in their jobs, and productivity and quality will improve.

Performance Assessment

Supervising with flexibility includes assessing the employee's performance level. Is the level below expectations (B), does it meet expectations (M), or does it exceed expectations (E)?

APPLYING A FLEXIBLE APPROACH

Motivation: **M** = Motivated, **LM** = Lacks Motivation
Skill: **S** = Skilled, **US** = Unskilled
Expectations: **B** = Below, **M** = Meets, **E** = Exceeds

Assess each employee using the chart below. Make a plan to improve performance as needed using either the Relationship Approach (RA) or the Training Approach (TA).

Goal or Other Measurement	Motivation M/LM	Skills S/US	Expectations B/M/E	Approach RA/TA

Strategies for Managing Performance

Review the strategies and put a check beside those that work best for you. Add the selected strategies to your action plans.

- ❑ **Hold a meeting with your work group**. Describe your excitement about the job, your desire to help, your expectations for positive results, and your goal to meet with each of them individually. Answer any questions and share any new company information. This is particularly helpful if you supervise former co-workers or friends.

- ❑ **Meet with each employee one-on-one for 15 to 20 minutes**. During that time, focus positively on:

  - ▷ Getting to know the individual or just talking about the job
  - ▷ Asking for help or suggestions from the employee
  - ▷ Reviewing your overall expectations
  - ▷ Outlining the goal-setting process

  Note: If you have 10 or more employees, do the above in small groups or identify team leaders to meet with employees. Take the time to train the team leaders in effective one-on-one communication skills.

- ❑ **Be available to employees**. Every day, observe your employees in action. Talk to them informally. Help out with job challenges if necessary. Be constructive. Be a good listener. Praise progress and offer encouragement. Observe areas that need improvement and begin identifying ideas where you can make positive changes.

- ❑ **Make an effort to work cooperatively with other groups or departments.** Get to know the other supervisors. Be a good listener and learn how your area can do a better job. Be positive and try not to get caught up in negative emotions or complaints.

- ❑ **Make necessary changes.** If the department is performing poorly, make changes more quickly. Be sure to talk the changes over with your boss first. Thoroughly explain the changes to your employees. If the group is performing well, make changes more slowly.

Part Summary

In this part we've talked about performance management. You've had a chance to review how to set SMART goals, how to ensure that your employees have the competence and motivation to do an effective job, and how to make sure that you're providing a positive climate that supports their initiative, personal responsibility, and commitment to do their job effectively. We've also discussed the importance of balancing your focus on the successful accomplishment of the task with an equally important focus on the relationship needed to foster ongoing effort and accomplishment.

P A R T 3

Communicating with Others Proactively

> "*By definition, communication means two-way communication. Insecure individuals don't like it. Bosses don't like it, but leaders and innovators do like it.*"
>
> **–Mark Shepard**

In this part:

- You'll focus on how to develop healthy, interdependent relationships with your team.
- You'll learn how to communicate effectively one-on-one, with your team and with your manager.
- You'll get a chance to learn how to delegate effectively.
- You'll get a chance to review your communication skills using a communications skills inventory.

Building Interdependent Relationships

There are two major kinds of human relationships:

- Dependent
- Interdependent

Dependent / Subordinate

Interdependent / Equal

In a dependent relationship, one person has most of the power and influence. Person A commands and B obeys. B is dependent on A for guidance, direction, support, and the latitude to act.

In an interdependent relationship more equality exists. Even though person A may have the authority or position power, she values B, and appropriately delegates responsibility, shares information, and allows B to fulfill the job without undue intrusion. In most relationships, which option is preferred?

An interdependent relationship is preferred because it builds trust, credibility, and rapport. To achieve excellence in supervision, you need interdependent relationships with employees. This type of relationship promotes the highest morale and productivity. Employees perform better because they *want* to.

Employees' perceptions of issues or problems often differ from a supervisor's. Unless the supervisor practices key communication skills, the different views can lead to conflicts. The conflicts can cause a lack of trust, resulting in diminished rapport and cooperation.

To counteract this, many supervisors resort to autocratic, "dependence producing" approaches to supervising. They act like a bull in a china shop. This may produce results in the short term but leaves a relationship mess behind. The byproduct of this type of autocratic leadership is employee ill will and low morale.

KEY COMMUNICATION SKILLS

Use this checklist to help you communicate more effectively. It will help you to develop interdependent relationships with employees. They will have better morale, productivity, and attitudes.

Rate yourself by circling the most appropriate number for each item. Add all circled numbers to determine your score. Then, put a plus sign next to three strengths and a check next to two areas that need improvement.

1 = Rarely 2 = Infrequently 3 = Sometimes 4 = Often 5 = Most of the Time

As a supervisor, I...

1. Take the time to communicate with others.	1	2	3	4	5
2. Listen to others' ideas, especially when I disagree.	1	2	3	4	5
3. Ask appropriate questions to gain more information.	1	2	3	4	5
4. Paraphrase my understanding of the issue.	1	2	3	4	5
5. Ask for input from others.	1	2	3	4	5
6. Acknowledge others' feelings, even if they are negative.	1	2	3	4	5
7. Treat others with respect and dignity.	1	2	3	4	5
8. Seek solutions that can be mutually agreed to.	1	2	3	4	5
9. Follow through on my commitments.	1	2	3	4	5
10. Follow up to ensure positive communication.	1	2	3	4	5
11. Pay attention through good eye contact and helpful body language.	1	2	3	4	5
12. Demonstrate that I care about others' situations or needs.	1	2	3	4	5

Total: __________

Key Communication Skills Scoring

If your score falls into the following ranges:

60–55

Excellent! You are on your way to great supervisory communication. Keep using these important skills, and keep learning!

54–44

You will benefit from further development. You are using many important supervisory skills. Stay focused and continue learning!

43 or below

You will benefit from immediate development. Select two to three areas of communication and make a concentrated effort to improve your use of these important supervisory communication skills. Make a commitment to keep learning!

"Someone better learn to delegate."

Communicating One-on-One with Employees

A large shipping company was having serious productivity problems. Employees felt like they were left "out of the loop" and they were concerned about a lack of communication. The supervisors in the company implemented a one-on-one policy. This meant that each supervisor met privately with each employee on a regular basis (twice a month) to maintain clear expectations, provide performance feedback, and coach as needed. Each supervisor met twice a year with each employee to review performance. Over time communication, morale, and productivity improved. This new approach helped the supervisors establish relationships with employees that reinforced their importance to the company and provided regular, effective communications to support problem-solving and feedback.

PURPOSE OF ONE-ON-ONE DISCUSSIONS

Earlier, we discussed the power of goals. The expectation and goal setting process requires one-on-one meetings with employees. Here are other ways to use the one-on-one process. Put a check next to the ones you have used:

- ❑ Discuss performance issues.
- ❑ Give recognition.
- ❑ Listen to personal problems.
- ❑ Conduct a coaching session.
- ❑ Solve problems.
- ❑ Brainstorm new ideas.
- ❑ Delegate a task.

Too often, supervisors won't take the time for one-on-one meetings because they are too busy. A *supervisor who is too busy for employees is too busy to be a supervisor*. Daily informal one-on-one meetings can be conducted in just a few minutes. Formal one-on-ones need to be done regularly and consistently (for example, from once a week to once a quarter, depending on the job). You should meet with inexperienced people more often. You should also meet more often if there is a sense of urgency for better results. These meetings usually take 30 to 60 minutes and will be described in more detail in the Part titled, "Coaching for Excellence."

Delegating Tasks

Excellent supervisors delegate. Bill Marriott Sr., chairman and CEO of Marriott International, said, "Don't do anything someone else can do for you." The goals of delegating are:

1. Give an employee a task she can do or can learn to do so you can accomplish other, more pressing goals (increase capacity).
2. Develop your employees' skills.
3. Accomplish better and faster results.

DELEGATING

Unfortunately, many leaders fail to delegate for a variety of reasons. Put a check next to any that apply to you. I sometimes don't delegate because:

- ❑ I lack confidence in employees' ability.
- ❑ I lack the time to communicate about a task or train an employee in the task.
- ❑ I take personal pride in doing a task myself.
- ❑ I have strong personal competence in a task and want it to be done right.
- ❑ I have a fear of letting go of a task.
- ❑ I don't know how to delegate.

How to Delegate

Meet with the employee one-on-one and follow these steps:

1. Outline clear expectations, goals, and reasons for delegating the task.
2. Set timelines for milestones and for completion.
3. Answer any questions or concerns.
4. Reassure the employee that he or she can do it. Give needed tools, support, or training.
5. Follow up to check on progress.

Remember, a supervisor's success depends on employees' success. As a general rule, delegate to more experienced employees. Learn to delegate tasks that matter to the organization but are hard for you to do because of other priorities. In addition, it is a great habit to periodically ask, "What am I doing right now that is really someone else's job? What am I doing now that someone else could do if trained and coached?" These questions will help to ensure that you're not slipping back into the role of an individual contributor. They help to ensure that you're not competing with your employees in the fulfillment of their jobs.

MAKING A PLAN TO DELEGATE

Briefly describe the tasks you're considering for delegation. Place a check in the appropriate box to indicate whether you should keep or delegate the task. Finally, write your reasons in the last column.

Task/Goal	Keep/ Delegate	Reason

Communicating with a Team

T ogether

E veryone

A chieves

M ore

Any time you supervise more than one person, teamwork issues can arise. All of the supervisory practices we have discussed will help build better teamwork. Another great tool for improving teamwork is to hold regular and effective meetings. The timing and frequency of the team meetings should be determined by its purpose and needs. Consider the examples below.

Poor Customer Service Ratings

A customer service department received poor survey ratings. To improve, the supervisor created a team of six customer service representatives to address this problem. Over a period of several months, the team met every week to identify the issues, discuss options, and create a plan. After implementing the plan to improve responsiveness and courtesy, the customer service ratings improved measurably.

Mediocre Financial Services Performance

A new supervisor for a financial services company felt it was important to improve communication in her department. Performance was mediocre, and the previous supervisor had been fired. The new supervisor instituted weekly department meetings to share information and work on problems. Within a few weeks, performance and morale increased significantly.

Use a Team Approach

Hold regular department or group meetings to:

- Share company and department information.
- Discuss problems.
- Recognize results.
- Conduct training.
- Create plans.
- Gain input.
- Review changes.
- Brainstorm ways to improve.
- Communicate about performance results.
- Check out how people are doing.

Guidelines for Team Meetings

Effective meetings are a direct result of good planning, preparation, and execution. Most regular weekly or monthly meetings will last 30 to 60 minutes. Whether your meeting lasts 30 minutes or 3 days, you must plan and prepare in order to make it a worthwhile use of talent and resources.

In all meetings:

- Be clear about your objectives. What do you want to accomplish?
- Prepare an agenda.
- Set clear ground rules or guidelines for participation.
- Keep a written record. Post topics and discussion points on a flip chart or white board so all participants have a view of the discussion and decisions.
- Start and end on time.
- Get others involved by asking for input and by letting others present material.
- Be a good listener.
- Publish the notes soon after the meeting.

The following page contains a worksheet to help you prepare for meetings. Make a copy and use it to prepare for your next meeting.

MEETING PLANNER

Department: ______________________ **Date**: ________________

Start Time: ______________ **End Time**: ______________

Agenda: Key Topics

1. ____
2. ____
3. ____
4. ____
5. ____
6. ____

Notes:

Communicating with Others

Jim was a superb supervisor and an excellent manager. When asked his secret, he replied with a smile, "Well, I didn't go to college." Then he laughed heartily! He added, however that his success was due to his ability to communicate. He started every day by greeting or talking to employees in his area and, if time allowed, in other departments. The discussion often focused on the employee's personal interests like their vacation, family, or general news. Jim said, "We only talked business if they brought it up." Over time, Jim developed strong and positive rapport with the employees.

Management guru Tom Peters coined the term "MBWA (Managing by Walking Around)." Get out where your employees are working. Make yourself available and roll up your sleeves to interact and work with your employees. This direct involvement builds trust, credibility, and rapport. It establishes and maintains the interdependent relationships that we discussed earlier.

Evidence of Poor Communication

Some common complaints employees have about supervisors' poor communication skills include the following. Place a check next to the ones you have experienced as an employee, and add another from your experience:

- ☐ The supervisor is never around to talk things over or make a decision.
- ☐ The supervisor is always in a meeting.
- ☐ The supervisor spends too much time on the computer pounding out memos or reports.
- ☐ The supervisor is unapproachable because of a negative attitude.
- ☐ The supervisor claims to always be too busy to discuss and listen to problems and concerns.
- ☐ The supervisor never holds a department meeting.
- ☐ Other: ______________________________

Communication requires interaction with others. It is an investment. If you give your employees more of your time, they will give you more of their effort. Treat people with respect, talk to them, listen, and work with them. If you do this, others will give you their best and they will go the extra mile.

Communicating with Your Manager

A CEO was asked the number one characteristic that he looked for in a supervisor. He responded by saying, "Initiative!" In other words, a supervisor needs to take action and make things happen. This also applies to communicating with your manager. Some managers do a great job; others do a poor job. Regardless, you need to effectively communicate upward.

Reasons for Communicating Upward

- Keep your manager informed of your progress.
- Build your manager's confidence in your ability to get things done.
- Minimize the problems your manager has to solve.
- Get help when needed.
- Share your ideas and solutions.

A new supervisor quickly discovered he had personnel problems. Three out of seven employees were performing poorly. He wasn't sure what to do. His manager was the "hands-off" type and wasn't particularly helpful. The supervisor talked to another manager to gain ideas to handle the performance issues. Then, he created a plan for improvement for each individual. After updating his manager on the problems and solutions, the manager said, "Sounds good; do it!"

COMMUNICATING POSITIVELY WITH YOUR MANAGER

Communicating with and influencing your manager is a critical skill set for an effective supervisor. Review the list of strategies below and check the items that you will focus on:

- ❑ Stay informed and be aware of what is going on in your area and around the company.
- ❑ Proactively seek ways to continuously improve.
- ❑ Don't bring problems to your manager—bring solutions (for example, "Here is a problem I'm having and this is what I plan to do about it.").
- ❑ Write goals and plans and talk them through with your manager, even if it isn't requested.
- ❑ Meet with your manager regularly (for example, weekly or monthly) to discuss your progress.
- ❑ Keep your manager informed about problems or changes. No surprises!
- ❑ Follow through on commitments and timelines. Stay organized to track these.
- ❑ Go out of your way to build positive bridges with other departments. Treat them as internal customers.
- ❑ Clarify priorities. Maintain focus on what's most important.
- ❑ Take responsibility. Don't blame others. If there are obstacles outside your control, identify ways to minimize them.

STRATEGIES FOR PROACTIVE COMMUNICATION

For each strategy, put a check beside the ones you will try. Add these to your action plans.

❑ **Make a commitment.** The Japanese use the term Kaizen, meaning "continuous improvement." Use this to focus on improving your communication. It's been said that "it's not your aptitude but your attitude that determines your altitude." Be willing to make improvement of your communication skills a lifelong process.

改善

❑ **Prepare, prepare, prepare.** Use the Meeting Planner worksheet to prepare for all your meetings. If you take the time to think things through, you will come across more positively, and you will appear more professional.

❑ **Ask for feedback.** Ask your boss or someone you trust to give you feedback on how well you communicate. Ask this person to rate you on the Key Communication Skills checklist. Listen to the feedback non-defensively.

❑ **Delegate tasks effectively.** Develop employees by delegating to them. This also helps you manage your time better. Delegate complex tasks with important priorities to more experienced people, and routine, less complicated tasks to less experienced people. Effective delegation requires a clear definition of the goal, standards, tasks, and timeline. Give training if needed. Don't ask someone to do a task and then look over his shoulder while doing it. This approach doesn't save time and employees resent it.

When an employee succeeds at the delegated task, give timely, specific, and positive feedback. If the employee does not complete the task successfully, take time to review the steps the employee took, assess the results, and discuss ideas for succeeding next time. Then give the employee another chance. Remember, one of the objectives of supervision is to accomplish more through the work of others. It is your job to coach and counsel employees toward success.

❑ **Read other books.** See the Additional Reading list in the Appendix for suggestions.

Part Summary

In this part we've discussed the importance of communicating to your employees—one-on-one and in teams. Your ability to establish productive, results-producing relationships that are based on mutual trust and respect rather than fear and position power will produce benefits for you and your employees. You've also had a chance to review some of the realities of delegating effectively and to get a "heads up" on some of the common barriers to effective delegations. Take advantage of the Additional Reading list and continue to improve your communication skills as you grow and develop as a supervisor.

PART 4

Coaching for Excellence

> *"A coach must keep everyone on the team in touch with present-moment realities—knowing where they stand, knowing where they're falling short of their potential, and knowing it openly and fairly."*
>
> -**Pat Riley, *The Winner Within***

In this part:

- You'll explore the changing world we operate within, and the impact it has upon us as supervisors.
- You'll examine the results of years of study and observations of the behaviors of the best and worst supervisors and managers.
- You'll get a chance to review your own coaching skills and determine areas for future growth and development for improvement.
- You'll take a look at formal and informal coaching practices and how and when to use them for your own effectiveness.

The Changing Playing Field

The playing field is changing in our world. Changes are driven by four key forces:

- Emergence of the Information Age
- Greater competition
- Increasing customer demands
- Volatile workforces

Emergence of the Information Age

- Emerging technology creates higher expectations for productivity and responsiveness.
- Ready availability and transmission of data creates information overload.

Greater Competition

- Business improvements and innovations
- Multinational consolidation
- Entrepreneurial spirit

Increasing Customer Demands

- More choices have emerged for customers.
- Customers want it all: price, quality, service.
- Word of mouth is faster via Internet.

Volatile Workforces

- Less employee loyalty
- Diverse workforces
- Varied generational needs
- Labor shortages

Because the playing field is changing, supervisors are under great pressure to do more with less. They are expected to be a liaison between employees and management, to increase productivity, to increase quality or service, and to build employee morale. To do this, many turn to the example set by those who serve in the role of coach—professional sports coaches, voice coaches, and mentors in all areas of personal and professional development.

While the challenges are great, supervisors who can adapt and learn to coach for better results become extremely valuable to their companies. Coaching is an essential skill for all supervisors. And, those who master it learn key behaviors and skills that produce immensely positive results.

"When we said 'get additional training', we didn't mean for the company softball team."

Coaching Behaviors in Supervisors

BEST AND WORST SUPERVISORS

Think of absolutely the worst supervisor you ever worked with or knew about. What did the person do? What was the person's character? Think of the best supervisor you worked for or knew about. How was this person different? In both cases, describe the coaching behaviors and character of the person. When complete, compare the behaviors you listed with those on the next page.

Worst Behavior	Character
1.	
2.	
3.	
4.	
5.	

Best Behavior	Character
1.	
2.	
3.	
4.	
5.	

Research in work settings has established that these are the coaching and behaviors of the least effective and most effective supervisors:

Most Effective Coaches	Least Effective Coaches
Establish clear expectations	Set unclear expectations
Set clear goals and standards	Set vague goals/standards
Give regular feedback	Give limited or vague feedback
Observe performance regularly	Observe performance irregularly
Give constructive feedback	Provide only negative feedback
Recognize and reward accomplishments	Give limited positive recognition
Provide regular training	Offer little training
Give helpful advice	Give sporadic advice
Invest the time to help	Spend more time on technical and administrative matters
Listen effectively	Listen ineffectively
Have good interpersonal skills	Have poor interpersonal skills

COACHING FOR EXCELLENCE INVENTORY

The behaviors of the best coaches translate into the practices below. Using the scale shown, rate how often you engage in the following behaviors.

1 = Never, 2 = Rarely, 3 = Sometimes, 4 = Often, 5 = Always

Be honest with yourself and answer as you think you really are, not what you would like to be:

____ 1. I discuss agreed-upon goals and expectations with my employees.

____ 2. I set aside uninterrupted and private time to meet with employees.

____ 3. I review my employee's goals and expectations at the start of each of my coaching sessions.

____ 4. I encourage open discussion when I hold coaching meetings.

____ 5. I ask employees for their input when reviewing their performance.

____ 6. I listen to and paraphrase what my employees are trying to say.

____ 7. I carefully assess all factors that affect employee performance results.

____ 8. I regularly observe employees in action with customers or others.

____ 9. I recognize and reward high performance.

____ 10. I give regular and immediate feedback to my employees in a constructive manner.

____ 11. I listen to employee feedback and concerns before giving my own.

____ 12. I am specific about behaviors and tasks when I give advice or guidance.

____ 13. I provide feedback that is appropriate to my employees' situations, performance levels, and goals.

CONTINUED

CONTINUED

____ 14. I teach my employees new skills clearly and systematically.

____ 15. I develop specific action plans to help improve my employees' skills and results.

____ 16. I gradually give more responsibility to employees so they can grow.

____ 17. I ensure that employees understand and agree to their action plans.

____ 18. I negotiate project tasks and deadlines with experienced employees.

____ 19. I set follow-up meetings at the conclusion of coaching meetings.

____ 20. I make sure that my follow-up coaching meetings take place.

Coaching for Excellence Inventory Scoring

Write in your score for each number in the space below. Put a plus sign by the top five numbers and a check by the lowest two. Then answer the questions.

Review Goals/ Expectations	**Assess Performance**	**Provide Feedback/ Guidance**	**Develop Action Plans**	**Establish Follow-Up**
1. ______	5. ______	9. ______	15. ______	19. ______
2. ______	6. ______	10. ______	16. ______	20. ______
3. ______	7. ______	11. ______	17. ______	
4. ______	8. ______	12. ______	18. ______	
		13. ______		
		14. ______		
Total:	**Total:**	**Total:**	**Total:**	**Total:**

How can you make sure you take the time to coach?

____

____

____

What are your strengths? (List 3–5.)

____

____

____

____

How can you coach even more effectively? (List 2–3 ways.)

____

____

____

The Coaching Process

There are two major types of coaching: formal and informal. Supervisors who embrace the coaching concept get more done in less time by helping the employees succeed. Coaching is the art of high performance. If you practice informal and formal coaching, employees may not like some of your decisions, but they will still respect you and get the job done.

Informal Coaching

Informal coaching involves the day-to-day relationship between the supervisor and the employee. First of all, is the relationship built on trust? All employees have what is called an emotional bank account. Author Steven Covey describes this in *The Seven Habits of Highly Effective People.* It is either positive or negative. If it is positive, trust is present, and results and performance are good. If it is negative, trust is absent, and performance often suffers.

Just as with a real savings account, an emotional bank account requires deposits before you make withdrawals. So how do you make the emotional bank account positive and increase trust? Think about what you would want from a supervisor.

Think about all the principles and practices we have discussed so far. Many of these points under informal coaching are examples of the techniques and strategies you have been working on. If these kinds of actions are everyday practices, you'll create a surplus in the emotional bank accounts of employees. This is crucial because, at times, you'll have to make the tougher decision: change work hours, require overtime, discipline an employee, follow through on an unpopular decision by management, or act in opposition to an employee's idea of what is best. These are withdrawals, often viewed negatively. With a surplus of positives in the emotional bank account, employees will stay motivated.

POSITIVE PRACTICES

- ❑ Greet the employee daily.
- ❑ Talk non-business matters of interest to the employee.
- ❑ Have lunch with employees.
- ❑ Demonstrate courtesy and respect.
- ❑ Learn and use people's names.
- ❑ Be a good listener.
- ❑ Have a sense of humor.
- ❑ Deal with performance issues.
- ❑ Do what you say you will do.
- ❑ Treat people fairly.
- ❑ Be considerate and understanding when dealing with personal matters.
- ❑ Be positive.
- ❑ Work side-by-side with employees on an important project.
- ❑ Encourage others.
- ❑ Give recognition for progress and results.
- ❑ Help out when necessary.
- ❑ Have some fun at work.
- ❑ Buy someone a soft drink or coffee.
- ❑ Other: ____

Formal Coaching

Formal coaching is talking one-on-one to help an employee improve performance. Coaching often involves a mutual problem-solving effort and it usually takes 30 to 60 minutes. Spending only a few minutes on a problem usually isn't formal coaching; it's more often giving direction—just telling the employee what to do!

Another goal of formal coaching is to develop the employees' skills at thinking through problems and identifying solutions on their own. Done successfully, in the future the employee will come to you with solutions to problems, rather than just the problems.

When is coaching the right management intervention? First, do it to help poor or marginal performers improve their performance. Second, do it to help a good performer excel or handle a difficult project. Third, use it in times of change. You have to schedule coaching sessions or you will never find time for them.

An office supervisor had an employee who generally met expectations, except for her accounts-receivable goal. She sometimes missed deadlines. After learning how to coach, the supervisor met with this employee weekly for 30 minutes. The coaching process and a skillful supervisor helped the employee adopt new project management practices and this positioned her to meet the goal. The employee added some ideas for the action plan that helped integrate all of her work. Afterward, monthly one-on-one goal meetings kept the employee on track.

Preparation

1. Set clear goals and expectations.
2. Identify the employee's skill, motivation, and performance level.
3. Do your homework and review the employee's current performance.
4. Set aside the time for a coaching meeting (30–60 minutes). Create a positive, friendly atmosphere.

The Coaching Process

1. Start the coaching session by clarifying the goal. Ask the employee to describe it as he or she understands it. Listen carefully to ensure that you and the employee have the same expectations for successful outcomes. If not, use this opportunity to clarify expectations.

2. Assess the current level of employee performance from employee input. Ask the four key questions below. You will ask other questions, but these are the core questions:

   ▷ Overall, how are you doing?

   ▷ What's working?

   ▷ What isn't working? If there are problems, explore the obstacles to successful performance and identify action steps to remove or overcome the obstacles.

   ▷ What can you do better or differently? Compare the employee responses to your observations and knowledge of their results.

3. Provide feedback and guidance. Comment on what the employee says.

4. Develop action plans with employee input. Give your ideas for the plan. Put the ideas for improvement in writing, add your recommendations, and gain agreement.

5. Establish follow-up steps. Summarize the discussion, and set a specific date and time for the next meeting.

6. Provide regular performance feedback. Use informal coaching strategies regularly

COACHING WORKSHEET SAMPLE

Name: Bill Jones   Date: 2/15

1. **Performance goals**: What is the key goal we are working on?
   - ▷ Improving the customer satisfaction rating to 95% or higher

2. **Assess performance**:

   Employee input: Supervisor will ask 4 key questions and take notes on employee comments.
   - ▷ Overall, how are you doing on this goal?
   - ▷ What strategies and actions are working well?
   - ▷ What isn't working?
   - ▷ What can you do better or differently?

   Observations/results: Supervisor, note your observations of performance and any available data, such as customer survey results.
   - ▷ Experiencing fewer complaints
   - ▷ Rating of 93.5 (last quarter)
   - ▷ Evidence that employee is following through on action plan

3. **Provide feedback/guidance**:
   - ▷ I would like you to make follow-up calls after customer contact.
   - ▷ I would also like you to send thank-you notes within one day after contact.

4. **Develop action plans**:

   Employee's ideas:
   1. Act more courteously—say please, thank you, and so on.
   2. Greet promptly—in less than 1 minute.

   Supervisor's ideas:

   3. Do follow-up calls—within two days.
   4. Send thank-you notes—daily.

5. **Establish follow-up steps**:

   Next meeting 2/28 at 3:00 p.m.

COACHING WORKSHEET

Name: ____________ Date: _____________

1. **Performance goals**: What is the key goal we are working on?

   ▷ ____

2. **Assess performance**:

   Employee input: Supervisor will ask 4 key questions and take notes on employee comments.

   ▷ ____

   ▷ ____

   ▷ ____

   ▷ ____

   Observations/results: Supervisor, note your observations of performance and any available data, such as customer survey results.

   ▷ ____

   ▷ ____

   ▷ ____

3. **Provide feedback/guidance**:

   ▷ ____

   ▷ ____

4. **Develop action plans**:

   Employee's ideas:

   ____

   ____

   Supervisor's ideas:

   ____

   ____

5. **Establish follow-up steps**:

   ____

   ____

Strategies for Effective Coaching

Review the strategies below. Put a check beside the ones you will attempt and add them to your action plans.

- ❑ **Discuss the results of the Coaching for Excellence Inventory with your manager or another supervisor.**

  During the review, talk about strengths and areas to improve. Brainstorm ideas. Discuss different ways to help employees. Resist the temptation to think that "this doesn't apply to our situation." Coaching works! Excellent supervisors everywhere make effective coaching a central element of their supervisory routine.

- ❑ **Review how you have applied informal coaching.**

  At the end of a work week, analyze what happened. What results did you achieve? Which employees had problems? Why? What worked? What didn't work? What can you learn or relearn from a review of your coaching activities this week? What will you do better or differently next week?

- ❑ **Complete a formal coaching session with an employee and document the results using the Coaching Worksheet in this book.**

  What did you learn? If you're comfortable, discuss the process with your manager or with another supervisor (peer). Remember to set high standards for yourself and continue practicing these skills and improving your own performance as a coach.

- ❑ **Reward yourself!**

  Becoming an excellent supervisor is not easy. Achieving excellence is difficult. Others, including your manager, may tell you not to waste your time coaching. There are obstacles. With persistence and determination, you'll experience the benefits—pride and self-satisfaction, as well as improved production and employee morale. So reward yourself! Go out to dinner, or enjoy a movie at home or at the theater.

Part Summary

In this part we've discussed the changing environment and the challenges it poses for supervisors in today's workplace. We've discussed best and worst practices of supervisors and managers. And, we've explored our personal coaching practices using the personal coaching inventory. In this part we've also explored formal and informal coaching procedures, and we've left you with both a sample of a recorded coaching session and the forms to guide you in holding your own coaching discussions with your employees.

PART 5

Dealing Positively with Change

To improve is to change, so to be perfect is to have changed.”

–Winston Churchill

In this part:

- You'll explore some of the most prominent sources of the overwhelming change that is impacting our organizations and our employees at a relentless, never-ending pace.
- You'll explore your role as a supervisor and a leader responsible to organize the efforts of your employees to get consistent, positive results as employees navigate through often uncharted terrain.
- You'll learn how to communicate, navigate, and manage change effectively.
- You'll also learn specific and useful skills to generate ideas and solutions, solve problems, and manage the process of making change happen proactively.

A New Paradigm

Humans are really change artists. Scientists say that every cell in a human body is replaced every five to seven years. Literally, a person is a different individual numerous times in life. If we tried to avoid this process of change we would die.

A few experiments can illustrate how most people handle change. Try these:

- Clasp your hands together. Notice which thumb is on top. Now clasp your hands with the other thumb on top. How does it feel?
- Fold your arms in front of your chest. Notice which arm is tucked in. Now fold the arms with the other arm tucked in. How does it feel?
- Write your name somewhere on this page, like you were signing a check. Now write your name again with your other hand. How does it look?

Most people handle change by resisting it. Did you try the three experiments? In the first two situations the change probably felt uncomfortable or weird. In the third situation, it was probably hard to write your name with the opposite hand. These are not unusual results. However, in the last scenario, if you no longer had your first hand, could you learn to write your name better with the other one? You could! Why? Because you have no choice. You would have to learn.

Earlier in this book we discussed the changing playing field. We outlined four forces that are driving change in our society. These forces are designing a new paradigm for the business world. They are creating a fast-paced, interdependent, dynamic marketplace. Organizations and people have to change to keep up. Change is the name of the game.

The Four Forces

- Emergence of the information age
- Greater competition
- Increasing customer demands
- Volatile workforces

Charles Darwin said, "It is not the strongest of the species that survive, nor the most intelligent…, but the one most responsive to change." How responsive or resistant are you to change? Do you see change as a problem or a possibility? There are two basic ways to change:

- **Proactive:** Make a deliberate choice and plan to change.
- **Reactive:** Change only when forced to.

We can't control everything that happens to us, so at times we will need to react to changes. However, we can always control how we respond to changes and determine proactive steps to accelerate the positive effect of changes.

THE REALITIES OF CHANGE

Think of a situation you have experienced where the difficulties of dealing with or managing change presented a major challenge to you.

1. What was the situation? ____________________

2. What changed? Why? ____________________

3. How did people react? Why? ____________________

4. What possible solutions presented themselves to you?

5. How did things work out? Then? Today?

6. What can you learn or re-learn from this experience?

Organizational Change

Our rapidly changing world creates tremendous pressure for companies to improve. Economist Joseph A. Schumpeler called the process of change in the economy "creative destruction." Old jobs fade away; new ones emerge. Old companies change or give way to new ones. Nearly half of all Fortune 500 companies in the 1980s are gone today. To survive, organizations must adapt. Companies have used a variety of approaches to change organizationally.

EXPERIENCING CHANGE

Put a check next to any of the following changes you have experienced:

___ Participative management
___ Action teams
___ Self-directed teams
___ Total quality management
___ Re-engineering
___ Creating a vision
___ The Learning Company
___ Restructuring
___ Decentralization/centralization
___ Employee involvement
___ Downsizing

___ New technology
___ Mergers/acquisitions
___ Company policy/benefit revisions
___ Reorganization
___ New product introductions
___ Relocation of offices/plants
___ New leadership
___ Strategic alliances
___ New performance standards
___ Layoffs
___ Other ______________________

The Impact of Change

During change processes, employees usually experience one or more of these effects:

- Lower morale
- Higher stress levels
- More conflicts and problems
- Decrease in productivity
- Decreased service or quality
- Poorer attitudes

As a supervisor, your challenge is to counteract these negative reactions. Your job is to lead employees through their resistance to higher performance levels. We will explore four techniques for handling change more positively:

Four Techniques

- Communicating change effectively
- Change-management skills
- Brainstorming
- Problem solving

To use these techniques well, you may need to change your perceptions of employee potential and your approach to getting things done.

Communicating Change Effectively

A supervisory group had to deliver some good and bad news to a large manufacturing company. The good news: Business was growing and orders were increasing. The bad news: Production needed to increase to meet demand, yet expenses had to be managed due to rising costs. In response to these pressures, management made a decision to change its policy of not requiring overtime in the summer. Temporary employees would be used where possible to minimize the impact on vacation plans, but the company had to hold the line on expenses. Therefore, some overtime would be required and some vacations would be cut short. Supervisors had to tell employees of this switch in policy just before the summer vacation season started.

One supervisor held a brief meeting and told employees of the policy change. She explained she didn't like it but she had to follow it. So, she said she didn't want any whining and presented the new schedule.

Another supervisor held a meeting and explained the change in policy. He empathized and listened to the employees' concerns. He gave details on why the company made the decision. He led the group in brainstorming how to implement the decision as fairly as possible. He acknowledged the late notice and recognized people for their contributions to their plan.

Which employee group do you suppose handled the change better? Obviously it was the second group. Why? The supervisor communicated change effectively.

Ten Steps for Implementing Change

1. Communicate specifics early and follow-up information regularly.
2. Include others ideas for the change if possible.
3. Describe changes in as much detail as you can.
4. Offer training to help with new skills or to overcome obstacles.
5. Listen to and acknowledge people's feelings and concerns.
6. Get all people involved to be accountable for the success of the change.
7. Brainstorm and focus on the "possibilities" of change.
8. Facilitate creative problem solving and planning.
9. Pay particular attention to those who have a difficult time with change.
10. Recognize and reward progress with implementation.

Techniques for Communicating Change

During a significant change, communicate beforehand, communicate during execution, and communicate about results. Elsewhere in this book, we described two approaches:

- Hold department meetings.
- Conduct one-on-one sessions.

To these we will now add three more:

- Use change-management skills.
- Get people involved through brainstorming.
- Do group problem solving.

These three will be described in the pages that follow.

Change Management Skills

During times of change you need to be aware of how individuals perform and how everyone works together. You need to communicate more, not less, during times of change. Another part of this book explains the acronym TEAM in terms of communication. It is a key to effective change management. TEAM also refers to strategies for managing change.

T **ogether** focus on a purpose of the change.

E **mpower** everyone to participate positively in adjusting to the change.

A **im** for consensus on how to achieve the goals of the change.

M **anage** the process to track more effective results.

The following table explains these strategies in more detail. Use it as a checkpoint to gauge the team efforts of your employees and determine what actions you can take to help them through the change. Highlight or underline key ideas as you review it.

Team Process	Employee Needs	Supervisor Behavior	Employee Behavior
Together focus on a purpose	Common goals Attention to content Leadership support	Interpret company goals Facilitate team's establishment of and buy-in to goals Evaluate and track progress toward goals Hold department meetings and one-on-one sessions	Clarify boundaries Ask questions to test own understanding Participate in making things better Help leader track and evaluate progress toward goals
Empower others to participate	High level of involvement/ communication Empathy Maintenance of self-esteem Leadership support Respect for differences Trust	Ask questions Listen to concerns, resistance Show understanding Summarize feelings about the situation Encourage people to move forward Encourage and support others	Contribute ideas Build on others' ideas Consider others' ideas Think creatively
Aim for consensus	Constructive conflict resolution Power within group to be involved in decisions Leadership support Trust Pride and self-satisfaction	Use group-process techniques (brainstorming, problem solving) Ask questions Listen Seek common interests Summarize Confront in constructive way	Focus on common interests and goals Encourage others to talk Listen to and consider others' ideas Make own needs known Disagree in a constructive way Summarize points
Manage the process	Attention to process Leadership support Trust Recognition	Give clear directions Intervene to keep everyone on track Read group and adjust Be positive Suggest alternative Communicate results Provide training	Listen Keep purpose Stay focused on objective Use own energy and enthusiasm to help process along Perform well

Brainstorming Change Ideas

An effective tool for gaining employee input, buy-in, and involvement in a change or improvement process is brainstorming. Brainstorming means you ask others to share ideas related to a task, goal, or change.

Guidelines for Brainstorming

- Go for quantity rather than quality, to keep ideas flowing.
- Absolutely no criticism is allowed.
- Everyone's participation is encouraged.
- Give people a few minutes to write individual notes.
- Share one idea at a time through a round robin or two.
- Build on each other's ideas.
- Move quickly.
- Creative or weird ideas are considered helpful.

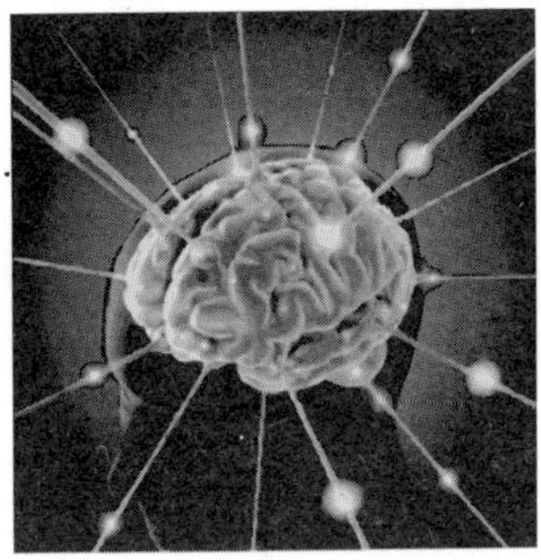

The Brainstorming Process

1. Set a predetermined time limit for sharing (5 to 15 minutes).
2. Pose a question such as: How can we implement this change positively?
3. Write all ideas on a flip chart or whiteboard. (Use the speaker's words.)
4. Read the list of ideas.
5. Ask what can be learned from this exercise.
6. Ask everyone to identify individually the top five to seven ideas.
7. Record votes for each idea. Identify the top ideas.
8. Review ways to implement various ideas.
9. Create plans to follow through.

USES OF BRAINSTORMING

Brainstorming can be used in other ways also. In this list, place a check beside one area you can apply it to, or add your own area.

- ❑ Improve a procedure.
- ❑ Increase quality/service.
- ❑ Build teamwork.
- ❑ Increase productivity.
- ❑ Other: ______________________________

Problem-Solving Techniques

Someone once said, "The more problems you have, the more alive you are." Without problems, there wouldn't be a need for supervisors. When confronted with problems, you need a problem-solving process.

The Problem-Solving Process

1. Clearly and specifically identify the problem.
2. Outline the most significant three to five obstacles that get in the way of success.
3. Outline three to five supportive forces that will help your success.
4. Identify three alternative solutions and the possible outcomes.
5. Decide on a course of action. (You may need to explore the other solutions later.)
6. Create a specific plan to implement the solution. Add timelines.

A sales supervisor had a new product to sell. After a couple of weeks results were poor. Because of the fast rollout of the product, minimal training was provided beforehand. After listening to some calls and talking to her reps, the supervisor used the problem-solving process to deal with the issue. Reps were divided into three groups to receive three short training sessions over a two-week period. The training focused on product knowledge and handling objections. Results improved dramatically.

Problem-Solving Practice

Identify a problem you are facing and use the Problem-Solving Process to help you improve. Whether or not you are facing change, this process can help you keep a positive attitude. In this era of fast-paced change, if you aren't getting better, you are getting worse. Always have goals and plans to move forward.

Problem Statement:

____

____

Obstacles:

____

____

Support:

____

____

Alternative Solutions:

A. ______________________________________

B. ______________________________________

C. ______________________________________

Recommended Solutions:

A. ______________________________________

B. ______________________________________

C. ______________________________________

Action Steps:

A. ______________________________________

B. ______________________________________

C. ______________________________________

STRATEGIES FOR MANAGING CHANGE

Review the strategies for managing change and put a check beside the ones you will try. Add these to your action plans.

- ☐ **Communicate changes positively.** As a supervisor you won't always be on the front end of organizational changes. Your job will often be to implement changes. Sometimes it won't be pleasant because it may mean procedural changes, downsizing, lay-offs, or cost controls. However, you can always communicate and demonstrate empathy. Use meetings and one-on-one sessions to gain ideas or allow people to vent feelings.

  The Ten Steps for Implementing Change remind you of how to make transitions more smoothly in your area. Although upper management may not always do this, you can! What two or three of the steps do you feel you can do well? What two or three steps do you need to remember to do better? Are you in the midst of change now? Which steps do you need to practice?

- ☐ **Apply change-management skills.** The TEAM chart shows you the behaviors you need to demonstrate, the needs of employees, and the involvement you want from employees. Where can you apply this today?

- ☐ **Conduct a brainstorming session.** Follow the process and follow up to use the ideas. Whether or not you are in the midst of massive change, use these techniques to gain employee ideas and commitment to improve results. Remember that most employees today want to feel they are a part of something—a team, cause, or purpose. You need their head and hands, but also their hearts.

- ☐ **Implement the Problem-Solving Process**. In Part 1: Getting Started, you created an action plan to prepare to win. How have things gone for you? What has worked well? What hasn't worked well? What will you do better or differently? Chances are you have some problems to solve. What's your biggest problem? Or, if things are going really well, where can you apply the continuous improvement approach? Use it, and you'll make more progress.

Part Summary

In this part we've discussed the difficult supervisory responsibility to guide and lead a team in times of continuous change. In fact, the job of a supervisor is to initiate change—to improve performance, generate higher quality, develop more capacity, and help employees reach for their highest potential. Without a doubt, your role as a supervisor fulfills the most important leadership role that your employees depend upon. Use the skills contained here to communicate, navigate, and lead your employees to stay current, take advantage of the continuous flurry of new technological tools, and flourish in the midst of the most amazing time of change that humankind has ever experienced.

APPENDIX

Action Plan: Keep Excelling

Listed below are all the suggested strategies in the book. Put a check beside the items you have accomplished. Then consider which additional strategies you'd like to focus on next; place an X next to those items. As you answer the questions that follow, make plans to incorporate these strategies into your Action Steps to help you achieve your goals.

Getting Started

- ❑ Obtain a copy of your job description (or create one).
- ❑ Talk to and interview three other supervisors or managers.
- ❑ Make a plan to thoroughly complete this book.
- ❑ Develop a written plan for your work area.
- ❑ Meet with your boss.

Managing for High Performance

- ❑ Hold a meeting with your employees.
- ❑ Meet with each employee one-on-one.
- ❑ Be available to employees.
- ❑ Work cooperatively with others.
- ❑ Make necessary changes.

Communicating with Others Proactively

- ❑ Make a commitment to keep learning.
- ❑ Prepare, prepare, prepare.
- ❑ Ask for feedback.
- ❑ Delegate tasks effectively.
- ❑ Read a communication book.

Coaching for Excellence

- ❑ Discuss the results of the Coaching for Excellence Inventory with your boss.
- ❑ Review how you have applied informal coaching.
- ❑ Complete a formal coaching with an employee.
- ❑ Reward yourself.

Dealing with Change Positively

- ❑ Communicate changes positively.
- ❑ Apply change-management skills.
- ❑ Conduct a brainstorming session.
- ❑ Implement the problem-solving process.

Assessing Yourself

Overall, what have you done well as a supervisor?

____

____

____

Overall, what hasn't worked very well for you?

____

____

____

What do you need to improve and do better as you look ahead?

____

____

____

Department Goals/Priorities

1. ____________________
2. ____________________
3. ____________________
4. ____________________
5. ____________________

Based on the goals and priorities above, what actions will you take and what is your timeline for completing them?

How Good Can You Be?

How good can you be? Scientists estimate that the average human being uses less than 10% of his or her potential. Unfortunately, too many supervisors use excuses like:

- I don't have time.
- Management doesn't support me.
- Employees don't care.
- Unions are too combative.
- Customers don't understand.
- I tried.

On and on the whine list goes and these supervisors forget to do what President Harry S. Truman said—"The buck stops here." When you are a supervisor, you are accountable and responsible. While there are obstacles, and some are very difficult, are these obstacles that hard, really?

Think of the Potential, Not the Problems

Cliff Miedl was a 20-year-old plumber's apprentice. While working on a job, he accidentally drove his jackhammer through three high-voltage cables. His body was hit with 30,000 volts of electricity. That's fifteen times the amount delivered by the electric chair. The jolt blew off most of his toes, shattered his knees, exploded part of his skull, and put a hole in his back as the electricity left his body. His heart stopped beating three times, yet he survived. Doctors said he'd never walk again.

Through a slow and painful recovery, he learned to walk again. Not only that, he was inspired by 1988 Kayak Olympian Greg Barton (who had club feet) who won two gold medals in Seoul, so he learned how to kayak. He became good at it and made the U.S. Olympic team. On opening night of the 2000 Sydney Games, the 603 members of the Olympic teams voted him the flag bearer for their march into the stadium. Cliff turned a tragedy into a triumph.

Receiving 30,000 volts of electricity is hard. The road back is hard. Absent employees or management policy changes can be difficult to deal with but not hard compared to Cliff's ordeal. So always believe in the potential—what you can do or control. Don't waste time on what you can't do or can't control.

Be Action Oriented, Not Apathetic

Supervisors are the single biggest influence on employees' performance according to Gallup Poll research. What an opportunity to make a difference! Too many supervisors give up, react negatively, or let events push them around. Take action!

A man earned a spot in the Guinness Book of World Records for running 90 marathons in a year. At the start of the new millennium, he ran 200 in 2000! When asked why, he replied he didn't want anyone to break his record and he knew he could do it. You don't need to run marathons unless you want to. As a supervisor, with the right actions—communication, goalsetting, recognition, coaching, and problem solving—you can motivate people toward superb results.

Stay Proactive, Not Reactive

It's been said, "All great achievers are great planners." You have to have a plan and then adjust the plan as needed. Scientists say the difference between a human being and a gorilla in terms of DNA is 2.8%. It's not much, but it matters. The key ingredient there is humans' ability to think.

The Human Genome Project is an effort to identify the human DNA map cell by cell. The significance of this evidence is that it changes medicine from a reactive discipline to a proactive one. Literally, scientists predict that if a baby has a predisposition for disease before it is born, doctors could switch the cells to be preventive. While there are many ethical concerns to debate about this, the fact remains that human intellect has discovered the technology to do this.

Again, this demonstrates the capacity of a person to identify and solve problems. That's an important part of a supervisor's job. Think! Then work with employees to achieve the goal. Never underestimate the ability of people to excel or your ability to succeed.

Viva-Crisp 50-Minute
Titles in the Series

ISBN	Author	Title	YOP	Price
9788130918174	Gambino	**50 Minutes to Better Software Demos**: *Apply Your Sales Skills with Confidence*	2011	195.00
9788130918488	Bozek	**50 One-Minute Tips to Better Communications**: *Speak, Write and Present More Effectively, 3/e*	2011	250.00
9788130918211	Conlow & Watsabaugh	**Achieving Supervisory Excellence**: *Be the Leader Your People Need*	2011	195.00
9788130918396	McKnight & Chapman	**Attitude**: *Protect Your Most Priceless Asset, 5/e*	2011	245.00
9788130918495	Terry Dickey	**Basics of Budgeting**: *Become a Better Business Planner, 2/e*	2011	250.00
9788130918310	Conlow & Watsabaugh	**Become a Successful Supervisor**: *Develop Essential People Skills*	2011	225.00
9788130918327	Brock	**Better Business Writing**: *Become A More Powerful Communicator, 5/e*	2011	225.00
9788130918228	Dupont	**Business Etiquette & Professionalism**: *Conduct Yourself With Confidence, 3/e*	2011	195.00
9788130918181	Morgan	**Calming Upset Customers**: *Stay in Control ... In any Situation, 4/e*	2011	195.00
9788130918198	Minor	**Coaching and Counseling**: *Become a Better Manager Through Mentoring, 4/e*	2011	195.00
9788130918273	Decker	**Communication Skills for Leaders**: *Deliver a Clear and Consistent Message, 4/e*	2011	225.00
9788130918143	Kindler	**Conflict Management**: *Resolve Disagreement at Work, 4/e*	2011	165.00
9788130918280	Conlow & Watsabaugh	**Creating a High Performance Team**: *Gain the Skills of Today's Successful Leaders*	2011	225.00
9788130918334	Feldman	**Critical Thinking**: *Make Strategic Decisions With Confidence, 2/e*	2011	225.00
9788130918426	Flynn	**E-Mail Management**: *Keep Your Inbox Under Control, 2/e*	2011	245.00
9788130918471	Kravitz & Schubert	**Emotional Intelligence Works**: *Think, Be and Work Smarter, 3/e*	2011	245.00
9788130918150	Maddux	**Ethics in Business**: *Manage With Authority and Fairness, 2/e*	2011	195.00
9788130918235	Rouillard	**Goals and Goal Setting**: *Achieve Measurable Results, 4/e*	2011	195.00
9788130918204	Conlow Watsabaugh	**Handling Difficult People and Situations**: *Lead People Through Adversity*	2011	195.00

ISBN	Author	Title	YOP	Price
9788130918433	Wendover	**High Performance Hiring**: *Select the Best Every Time, 3/e*	2011	245.00
9788130918402	Shea	**Making the Most of Being Mentored**: *Mentors Help Mentees Do, 2/e*	2011	245.00
9788130918242	Scott	**Managing Personal Change**: *Stay Positive and Stay in Control, 3/e*	2011	195.00
9788130918341	Haynes	**Meeting Skills for Leaders**: *Make Meetings More Productive, 4/e*	2011	225.00
9788130918440	Shea	**Mentoring**: *Make It A Mutually Rewarding Experience, 4/e*	2011	245.00
9788130918525	Shandler	**Motivating the Millennial Knowledge Worker**: *Help Today's Workforce Succeed in Today's Economy*	2011	395.00
9788130918167	Mandel	**Presentation Skills**: *Captivate and Educate Your Audience, 4/e*	2011	195.00
9788130918518	Pokras	**Problem Solving for Teams**: *Make Consensus More Achievable, 3/e*	2011	295.00
9788130918259	Haynes	**Project Management**: *Get from the Idea to Implementation Successfully, 4/e*	2011	195.00
9788130918372	Martin	**Quality Customer Service**: *Satisfy Customers– It's Everybody's Job, 5/e*	2011	245.00
9788130918457	Lightle & Doucet	**Sexual Harassment in the Workplace**: *Create a Better Workplace For Everyone, 3/e*	2011	245.00
9788130918501	Lengefeld	**Study Skills Strategies**: *Get the Most From Every Minute of Learning, 4/e*	2011	250.00
9788130918358	Conlow & Watsabaugh	**SuperSTAR Customer Service**: *It's all about C.A.R.E.*	2011	225.00
9788130918297	Maddux & Wingfield	**Team Building**: *Turn Personal Strengths Into Group Success, 5/e*	2011	225.00
9788130918464	Finch	**Telephone Courtesy & Customer Service**: *Be Your Company's Lifeline to Customers, 4/e*	2011	245.00
9788130918389	Conlow & Watsabaugh	**Telephone Skills that Satisfy Customers**: *Unleash the Full Potential of the Telephone*	2011	245.00
9788130918303	Romero	**The Business of Listening**: *Become a More Effective Listener, 4/e*	2011	225.00
9788130918365	Chapman & McKnight	**The New Supervisor**: *Lead With Confidence, 5/e*	2011	225.00
9788130918266	Haynes	**Time Management**: *Get An Extra Day a Week*	2011	195.00
9788130918419	Gill & Chatton	**Understanding Financial Statements**: *Master the Tools That Help You Succeed, 3/e*	2011	245.00